CELEBRATING THE FAMILY NAME OF MUÑOZ

Celebrating the Family Name of Muñoz

Walter the Educator

Silent King Books
a WhichHead Entertainment Imprint

Copyright © 2024 by Walter the Educator

All rights reserved. No part of this book may be reproduced in any manner whatsoever without written permission except in the case of brief quotations embodied in critical articles and reviews.

First Printing, 2024

Disclaimer

This book is a literary work; the story is not about specific persons, locations, situations, and/or circumstances unless mentioned in a historical context. Any resemblance to real persons, locations, situations, and/or circumstances is coincidental. This book is for entertainment and informational purposes only. The author and publisher offer this information without warranties expressed or implied. No matter the grounds, neither the author nor the publisher will be accountable for any losses, injuries, or other damages caused by the reader's use of this book. The use of this book acknowledges an understanding and acceptance of this disclaimer.

Celebrating the Family Name of Muñoz is a memory book that belongs to the Celebrating Family Name Book Series by Walter the Educator. Collect them all and more books at WaltertheEducator.com

USE THE EXTRA SPACE TO DOCUMENT YOUR FAMILY MEMORIES THROUGHOUT THE YEARS

MUÑOZ

Through the winding roads of time, the name Muñoz has grown,

Celebrating the Family Name of

Muñoz

A legacy of courage, in every seed that's sown.

From mountain peaks to valleys deep, their stories stretch afar,

A family bound by strength and pride, as constant as a star.

In lands of sun and ancient soil, the Muñoz name took root,

With hands that worked the earth and sky, a rhythm resolute.

Through seasons wild and winds untamed, they carved their path with grace,

Their hearts held firm, their eyes alight, a fire time won't erase.

Each generation, like a flame, passed down with love and care,

In every dream, in every step, their legacy is there.

From fields of gold to city streets, wherever they may go,

The name of Muñoz whispers bold, its presence like a glow.

The Muñoz heart is forged in strength, in loyalty and kin,

Celebrating the Family Name of

Muñoz

With every bond they make, the circle widens from within.

Their laughter rings like silver bells, their love, a quiet song,

In times of joy or trials faced, they know where they belong.

Through centuries of changing winds, they've held their heads up high,

A family that the world can see, like eagles in the sky.

No challenge too immense to face, no storm too fierce to stand,

The Muñoz name, a beacon bright, across the changing land.

Their roots run deep, as rivers flow, their branches spread so wide,

With stories etched in every soul, and honor as their guide.

From the old world to the new, they carry all that's true,

With every step, the Muñoz way shines through in what they do.

Their name is whispered on the breeze, it dances with the rain,

In fields of wheat and city lights, it carries no disdain.

For every life they touch and change, for every road they pave,

The Muñoz strength, enduring still, in every heart engraved.

Celebrating the Family Name of

Muñoz

With hands that build and minds that dream, they shape the world anew,

A family forged in unity, in loyalty so true.

No matter where the journey leads, no matter what they face,

The Muñoz spirit stands aloft, a testament to grace.

So let the winds of time blow on, let history be told,

Of Muñoz hearts that never wane, of Muñoz souls so bold.

For in each heart that bears this name, a light forever glows,

A symbol of a strength passed down, a legacy that grows.

Celebrating the Family Name of

Muñoz

From sunlit dawns to twilight's end, they stand the test of time,

The Muñoz name, a song of love, forever in its prime.

And as the future opens wide, their path will still be clear

The Muñoz way will carry on, with every coming year.

ABOUT THE CREATOR

Walter the Educator is one of the pseudonyms for Walter Anderson. Formally educated in Chemistry, Business, and Education, he is an educator, an author, a diverse entrepreneur, and he is the son of a disabled war veteran. "Walter the Educator" shares his time between educating and creating. He holds interests and owns several creative projects that entertain, enlighten, enhance, and educate, hoping to inspire and motivate you. Follow, find new works, and stay up to date with Walter the Educator™

at WaltertheEducator.com

Milton Keynes UK
Ingram Content Group UK Ltd.
UKHW020047181024
449757UK00011B/558

9 798330 468577